I Want To Marry You

A manual on the biblical principles of marriage

Pastor Chris Ojigbani

xulon
PRESS

Pastor Chris Ojigbani
Covenant Singles and Married Ministries
No 2 Admiralty Road, Lekki Phase I
P.O. Box 70351, Victoria Island,
Lagos, Nigeria
Tel: +234 1 850 5522, +234 802 717 3678
Website: www.singlesandmarried.org

Printed in the United States of America

ISBN 1-59781-847-X

www.xulonpress.com

Dedication

To the Glory of God

Table of Contents

Introduction

A forty-two year old Christian met a lady he wanted to marry. He proposed to her, she accepted and they made their intention known to the marriage council of their local church. Thereafter, they started courtship. The man, planning a strong financial base for his would-be family, provided his fiancée with money for a business. When the church marriage council heard that the man was responsible for bankrolling the lady's business, they cancelled the proposed marriage. The church marriage council's reason for cancelling the marriage was that the money the man gave to his fiancée must have influenced her decision in accepting to marry him. The council felt that the lady's acceptance to marry the man might be based on money and not on true affection.

A few years later, the man met another lady he wanted to marry. He proposed and the lady accepted. Again, when the church marriage council found out that he bought a gift for his fiancée, their courtship was cancelled. He finally got married to another lady, several years later, at the age of 50. Is it the will of God that the man should experience such setbacks or delays in getting married?

Now, what about the Christian lady in her forties? Beautiful, well behaved, yet single! What about the Christian brother in his forties? He is handsome, has a good paying job, but single. Is it God's desire that some people should experience setbacks and delays in getting married?

Without doubt, it is definitely not God's desire that His children should find it difficult to get married. His desire is that every adult should be married. How do I know this? By the statement God Himself made in the book of Genesis.

And the LORD God said, It is not good that the man should be alone; I will make him an help meet for him.

(Genesis 2:18)

Because of God's strong desire for every adult to get married, He gives a reward for marriage.

> *Whoso findeth a wife findeth a good thing, and obtaineth favour of the LORD.*
>   (Proverbs 18:22)

The reward God gives for marriage is favour. God uses the reward of favour to motivate people to get married. For God to be motivating people to get married indicates first, that He has a strong desire for every adult to get married; and second, that there should be no difficulty in getting married.

If it is God's desire that all His children should get married without difficulties, why then do some Christians get married late? Why do many marriages break up? Why has the traditional system of marriage in the Bible been neglected and considered outdated in this generation while subjects like holiness, prosperity, healing and faith are still regarded as relevant, and are being taught in accordance with the scripture?

All of these happen as a result of the devices of the devil. The devil does not want marriages to hold. He prefers late marriages, single parenthood, separation and divorce. Over the years, the devil has injected into the minds of people (including Christians), lots and lots of conditions and criteria for marriage. I want to let you know that being a born-again Christian does not stop the devil from injecting thoughts into you. That is why the Bible says we should guard our hearts with all diligence. The devil injected thoughts into Eve in the Garden of Eden, when she had a sinless heart.

> *But I fear, lest by any means, as the serpent beguiled Eve through subtlety, so your minds should be corrupted from the simplicity that is in Christ.*
>
> (2 Corinthians 11:3)

If the devil could do it to Eve then he could do it to any believer.

The conditions and criteria for marriage, which the devil has injected into the minds of people, have made it difficult for many people to get married. Knowing that Christians would no longer experience difficulty in finding a spouse and enjoying their marriages if they understand the biblical principles of marriage, the devil does everything possible to make Christians misunderstand it. In your own case, it is too late for the devil. That you are reading this book is an indication that God wants you to understand the biblical principles of marriage. He wants you to have a sound and successful marriage.

This book is written to eradicate all wrong doctrines and criteria of marriage, which cause difficulties and delays in getting married. In this book, I have exposed all the devices of the enemy that cause late marriages, thereby making it very easy for you to find and get married to your right spouse. This book will also feed you with enough biblical principles that will enable you to have a successful and enjoyable marriage.

To achieve this, I have used the scripture as the basis for separating non-Bible based doctrines of marriage from the Bible based doctrines. This is in accordance with the scripture being our manual of instruction.

> *All scripture is given by inspiration of God, and is profitable for doctrine, for reproof, for correction, for instruction in righteousness.*
>
> (2 Timothy 3:16)

CHAPTER ONE

The Purpose of Marriage

What is marriage?

Marriage is a life union between a man and a woman. It is the best, sweetest and most important union on earth. Because of its importance, God Himself instituted and conducted the first marriage in this world.

> *Therefore shall a man leave his father and his mother, and shall cleave unto his wife: and they shall be one flesh.*
> (Genesis 2:24)

The mystery of marriage

When a marriage takes place, there is a fusion of the man and the woman. This fusion makes them one flesh. **They are two individuals, yet one flesh.** The scripture calls it a mystery.

For this cause shall a man leave his father and mother, and shall be joined unto his wife, and they shall be one flesh.

This is a great mystery: but I speak concerning Christ and the church.
                                    (Ephesians 5:31-32)

The ordinary mind cannot comprehend the fusion of a man and a woman in marriage. It is a great mystery. This union of man and woman increases the spiritual strength of the couple. The Bible, speaking in Deuteronomy 32:30, says that one shall chase 1,000 and two shall chase 10,000. Instead of chasing 1,000 as they were as individuals before their marriage, together they shall chase 10,000 when they are married. The fusion of the man and the woman in marriage makes their spiritual strength increase to such an extent that nothing can be impossible for them to achieve.

And the LORD said, Behold, the people is one, and they have one language; and this they begin to do: and now nothing

*will be restrained from them, which they
have imagined to do.*

(Genesis 11:6)

Once the couple is united, the fusion produces a spiritual force that will make it impossible for anything to restrain them from achieving
whatever they have *imagined* to do. **When a
couple is united, there is no force strong
enough to stop them from achieving any of
their desires**. This means that all the couple's
desires, including the fruit of the womb, good
health, prosperity and longevity will become ful-
filled in their lives if they are united.

Because the devil cannot restrain any couple
from achieving their hearts' desires unless they
are disunited, his focus is to cause disunity
among couples. This divide-and-rule tactic of
the devil is the major weapon he uses against
marriages.

*Wherefore they shall no more be twain,
but one flesh. What therefore God hath
joined together, let no man put asunder.*

(Matthew 19:6)

The fusion in marriage is so perfect that nothing can separate the couple. Trying to separate

them can only lead to their destruction because they are already one. God does not support separation at all. God hates divorce. *I hate divorce, says the LORD God of Israel* (Malachi 2:16).

The primary purpose of marriage

The primary purpose of a thing must be established before the creation of that thing. Primary purpose implies the original intention for creating a thing. This means that after the creation of the thing, other purposes that it may serve become secondary. No matter how important those other purposes may be; they remain secondary.

If a man in need of stamping his official documents produces an inkpad, then the primary purpose of producing the inkpad is for stamping his documents. If after the production of the inkpad, the man then uses it for thumb printing, the primary purpose of producing the inkpad still remains stamping of documents. In as much as you can say that thumb printing is one of the purposes of the inkpad, it is secondary because it emanated after the production of the inkpad.

The primary purpose of a thing is the original reason for creating it. In this case, it means the foremost reason why marriage was founded.

Raising godly children, which is one of the purposes of marriage is secondary because it was derived after the creation of marriage itself.

> *And did not he make one? Yet had he the*
> *residue of the spirit. And wherefore one?*
> *That he might seek a godly seed...*
> (Malachi 2:15)

It is clear from the above scripture that one of the purposes of marriage is to have godly offspring. Though this purpose of marriage is very important, it is still secondary.

Another important secondary purpose of marriage is to have legitimate sex.

> *I say therefore to the unmarried and*
> *widows, It is good for them if they abide*
> *even as I. But if they cannot contain, let*
> *them marry: for it is better to marry than*
> *to burn.*
> (1 Corinthians 7:8-9)

The Bible says here that if anyone cannot abstain from sex, let him or her marry. That way, he or she can have sex legitimately. This purpose of marriage is important but because it emanated after the creation of marriage, it is secondary.

There are many other purposes of marriage but there is only one primary purpose of marriage. It is the original reason why marriage was instituted. The primary purpose of marriage is to have *an help meet* to help you fulfil your purpose in the kingdom of God. This primary purpose was determined before the creation of marriage itself.

> *And the LORD God said, It is not good that the man should be alone; I will make him an help meet for him.*
>
> (Genesis 2:18)

In the above passage lies the primary purpose of marriage. Before this time, there was no woman and there was no marriage. First, God saw that it is not good for a man to be alone. Secondly, He also decided to make *an help meet* for him. When we know what *help meet* means and what the *help meet* would assist Adam to do, then we will see the primary purpose of marriage.

The word *help meet* is derived from the Hebrew word *ezer*, which means aid. Aid, according to the BBC English Dictionary is "something that makes things easier to do." Now, the question is what was Adam doing that needed aid? The only assignment God gave

Adam after creating him was to dress and keep the garden.

> *And the LORD God took the man, and put him into the Garden of Eden to dress it and to keep it.*
>
> (Genesis 2:15)

The assignment given to Adam in the above passage was the only thing he was doing until God, in verse 18 of Genesis 2, decided to get aid for him. This suggests that what the Bible means by *help meet for [Adam]* is an *aid* to help him dress and keep the garden - to aid Adam in fulfilling his assignment in the Garden of Eden.

Therefore, you can rightly say that the primary purpose of marriage in this generation is to aid you in fulfilling your purpose in the kingdom of God. In this generation, the kingdom of God can be likened to the Garden of Eden. When Adam sinned, man was driven out of the Garden of Eden. But our Lord Jesus Christ redeemed us and translated us back into the kingdom of God.

> *Giving thanks unto the Father, which hath made us meet to be partakers of the inheritance of the saints in light: Who hath delivered us from the power of dark-*

*ness, and hath translated us into the king-
dom of his dear Son: In whom we have
redemption through his blood, even the
forgiveness of sins.*

(Colossians 1:12-14)

**The primary purpose of marriage is to
help you fulfil your assignment in the kingdom of God.** In as much as there are other purposes of marriage, the original reason for
creating marriage is to help you fulfil your
assignment in the kingdom of God.

CHAPTER TWO

Understanding the True Meaning of Love

Importance of love

*L*ove is the major ingredient for a successful marriage. **It is such that when you are operating in love and your spouse is not, your marriage cannot break up.** Just one of the couple's love is enough to sustain a marriage. If Christians understand and practise true love, there will be no more separation or divorce in Christian marriages.

Many Christians do not understand the true meaning of love and as such cannot practise it. Simply put, you cannot do what you do not know. The devil has seriously attacked the church of Christ in the area of love for many years. The devil's deceit is such that many Christians today practise wrong doctrines of love.

In this chapter, you will come to understand the true meaning of love, which will empower you with the required knowledge to have a successful and enjoyable marriage.

What is love?

Love is a sacrificial action for another who does not deserve it. This definition of love is completely based on the scripture. Love is an action and not an emotion or feeling. The world's love, which is based on emotions and feelings, is reciprocal. The world gives love only where there is something to gain. The world's love is give and take – it has to be deserved. True love does not need anything in return. When true love is in place, it is not earned; it is not deserved. True love is based on the commitment of will and not on emotions and feelings.

How to recognise true love

There are two basic factors that must be in place in identifying true love. First, there must be a sacrificial action; and second, it must be unmerited. For better exposition, let me make reference to an example of true love in the Bible.

> *For God so loved the world, that he gave his only begotten Son, that whosoever believeth in him should not perish, but have everlasting life.*
>
> (John 3:16)

From the above passage, we see that because of God's love for us, he *gave* his only begotten son. The sacrificial action that expresses God's love in the passage is *His giving His only begotten son.* To identify love, there must be a sacrificial action. It does not necessarily mean material or financial sacrifice, but something must be forgone in order to satisfy another. In the book of John, you will see another instance where love is expressed by a sacrificial action.

> *Greater love hath no man than this, that a man lay down his life for his friends.*
>
> (John 15:13)

Our master, Jesus Christ, says in the passage above that there is no greater love than a man laying down his life for his friends. The sacrificial action in this case is *a man laying down his life for his friends* – a man sacrificing his own

27

life for his friends. To identify love, there must be a sacrificial action. The scripture also explains the same thing in the book of Romans.

> *But God commendeth his love toward us, in that, while we were yet sinners, Christ died for us.*
>
> (Romans 5:8)

In the scripture above, the sacrificial action that expresses our Lord's love for us is *Christ dying for us*. There must be a sacrificial action for you to recognise love. Contrary to many views that love is a feeling or an emotion, it is a sacrificial action.

Is it every sacrificial action that connotes love? No! It is love only when the sacrificial action is for another who does not deserve it. No matter the extent of sacrifice for another, it cannot be regarded as love unless the person does not deserve it. Even if you give all your belongings to another, it does not signify love unless the person does not merit it.

> *If I give all I possess to the poor and surrender my body to the flames, but have not love, I gain nothing.*
>
> (I Corinthians 13:3 NIV)

The above scripture indicates you can give all your possessions to the poor without implying love. It is not every sacrificial action that implies love. Sacrificial action can only be regarded as love when it is for another who does not deserve it. For a better illustration, let us revisit the book of Romans.

But God commendeth his love toward us, in that, while we were yet sinners, Christ died for us.

(Romans 5:8)

From the above scripture, we see that because of our Lord's love for us, He died for us and paid for our sins while we were still sinning against Him. This is true love. True love is not based on merit. For our Lord to have died for us while we were still sinning against Him shows that His love was not based on our merit. We did not merit the death of Christ at all. Just like grace is defined as an unmerited favour, **love is an unmerited sacrificial action.** When it is merited, it is no more love; you are only giving back what you received. Because love is not merited, it is based on a commitment of will and not on emotions or feelings.

Let us examine the following scenario. A

man meets an attractive lady and sleeps with her. Then he showers her with gifts and money. This is not love. The shower of gifts and money is merited. The day the lady becomes unattractive to the man is the same day he stops giving her gifts and money. In fact, he will stop seeing her. This is not love because the gifts and money given to the lady are based on emotions and feelings. She deserves the gifts and money because she is attractive to the man, and she sleeps with him. So the man actually gives back what he receives from her. That is why the man would stop the gift and even stop seeing her the very day she stops being attractive to him. This is not love. True love does not fail. Because the person does not deserve it from the onset, true love can never fail. That is why the Bible says *love never fails* (1 Corinthians 13:8 NIV)

Emotions and feelings can accompany love, but what makes an action love is when it is based on a commitment of will and not on merit. Emotions and feelings would always fail but love based on the commitment of will never fails.

If a man for instance after enjoying a good meal prepared by his wife buys her a gift, it is not love because she deserves it. It is nice buying her a gift, but this is not love because he is only giving her the gift in response to the good

food she prepared for him. Any person, including an infidel, can be nice to anyone who is nice
to him.

> *For if you love them which love you, what*
> *reward have you? do not even the publi-*
> *cans the same?*
>
> (Matthew 5:46)

Your being nice can only imply love when it
is not deserved. If a man buys a gift for his rude
wife, it implies love because she does not
deserve it. If a woman treats her rude husband
with respect and continues to show him kindness
in spite of his rudeness to her, it is also love. In
true love, no matter what either of the couple
does wrong, the other will forgive and recipro-
cate by doing good. The love would cover all the
wrong doings. That is why the Bible says *love
covereth all sins* (Proverbs 10:12). The sacrificial action is not based on his or her spouse's
merit. **This actually makes it impossible for
such marriage to break up even when only
one of the couple understands love, because
he or she will continue forgiving and doing
good no matter how long the other continues
offending him or her.**
Love is not having an emotion or a feeling

towards somebody. Emotions can accompany love but love is a sacrificial action for another who does not deserve it.

How should a Christian love?

The Greek Language has many different terms for love: God's love (agape), the love of brother (philadelphia), the love of parents (philostorgos), the love of children (philoteknos), friendship (philia), emotional or affectionate love (phileo) and so on. However, as Christians, we are expected to love only in one way, by sacrificial action for another who does not deserve it.

> *Husbands, love your wives, even as Christ also loved the church, and gave himself for it.*
>
> (Ephesians 5:25)

The Bible does not only tell husbands to love their wives but also tells them how to love: as Christ loved the church and gave himself for it. In as much as there exists what we call emotional or affectionate love, the Bible passage above says that every husband who is a Christian must love his wife as Christ loved the church and gave himself for it. Remember that Christ died for us when we were in sin, when we did not deserve it. This means that every husband must act sacrificially to his wife even when she sins against him or does what he dislikes.

Jesus Christ himself also commanded us that our love must be as he has loved us.

> *This is my commandment, That ye love one another, as I have loved you.*
> (John 15:12)

Our master Jesus Christ says that we must love only as he loved us. How did he love us? He died for us when we did not deserve it. That means that what Jesus Christ is saying in the passage above is that every Christian should love by sacrificing for another who does not deserve it. No matter the types of love that exist, as a Christian, you must only love as Jesus Christ loved us: by a sacrificial action for another who does not deserve it.

Who is qualified to love?

Is everybody qualified to love? No! Only true believers can love. It takes the spirit of God to love. For God is love. God and love are inseparable. You must have a relationship with God before you can love.

> *Beloved, let us love one another: for love is of God; and every one that loveth is born of God, and knoweth God. He that loveth not knoweth not God; for God is love.*

(1 John 4:7-8)

Without the spirit of God you cannot love. Love is not ordinary. You must know God to be able to love. For love is God. If you are not born again or you wish to renew your relationship with God, please pray this prayer from the depth of your heart.

Heavenly Father, I come before you this day as a sinner.
Please forgive me my sins.
I believe that Jesus Christ died for my sins
And on the third day, He resurrected.
I believe that Jesus Christ is my Lord, Saviour and Master.
Father, please remove my name from the Book of Death
And write my name in the Book of Life.
Give me the grace to carry on as a born again

Christian.

All these I ask and thank you in the mighty name of Jesus Christ, Amen.

As you have prayed this prayer from the depth of your heart, I congratulate you. Please go to a pastor in a living church near you to pray with you and get you rooted in God's Word.

Must you love your spouse before marriage?

One of the biggest problems singles have in the choice of their spouse is trying to find the one they love. This has led to a lot of late marriages, and some are still not married. It is a device of the devil to cause late marriages and single parenthood. A believer meets a lady he likes. She is beautiful and a true born again. Instead of marrying her, he tells you he does not *love* her. The *love* being referred to here is emotional *love* and not the true love. Please understand that true love is not a feeling or an emotion but your sacrificial action for another who does not deserve it.

Strong emotions may accompany true love, but it is the commitment of will that does not fail. There is nothing wrong with emotions but it is dangerous when your marriage is based on emotions. Any marriage that is based on emotions or feelings would always fail. For instance, a man who marries a lady because he is emotionally attracted to her slim shape and flat tummy is making a big mistake. Because after a few years or after she may have given birth, her wonderful shape and flat tummy will change. When that happens, the man will no longer be happy with the marriage because his reason for marrying her, which is her wonderful shape and flat tummy, is no longer there. **Emotions will always change, and may lead to frustration and probably separation.**

Because emotional *love* varies, it is not wise to rely on it as a basis for marrying somebody. On the other hand, it is also not wise to rely on emotional *love* as a basis for **not** marrying somebody. Because emotional love changes, you may not be emotionally attracted to someone today, but you may become attracted to the same person tomorrow. That is the reason why somebody may be emotionally attracted to a person at first sight, and it may take some time to develop emotional *love* towards another person. Emotional *love* cannot be relied on; it varies, and as such cannot be a reason for marrying or for not marrying somebody.

Though, it is not wrong to have emotional

love towards your spouse before marriage, I have to let you know that you can also marry your spouse and develop emotional *love* towards her or him after the marriage. Isaac married Rebekah before he developed emotional *love* towards her.

> *Then Isaac brought her into his mother Sarah's tent, and took Rebekah, and she became his wife; and he loved her: and Isaac was comforted after his mother's death.*
>
> (Genesis 24:67)

From the above passage, you will see that Isaac married Rebekah before loving her. *Loved* as in the above passage is derived from a Hebrew word, *ahab*. *Ahab* according to the New Strong's Exhaustive Concordance of the Bible means affectionate or sexual love. This means that Isaac's affectionate or emotional *love* towards Rebekah began after their marriage. The fact is that Isaac couldn't have *loved* Rebekah before the marriage because he saw her face only after the marriage. If God directs your steps to your intended spouse who is a true believer, and you like the person, please go ahead and marry him or her. Emotional *love* is not a criterion for choosing a spouse. In subsequent chapters, you will fully understand the scriptural conditions for marrying a right spouse.

CHAPTER THREE

Courtship

~~~~~~~~~~~

Courtship is a doctrine that is practised by both believers and unbelievers. The question is has courtship been beneficial or harmful to believers? Is it a biblical doctrine? How did it start? Of what purpose is courtship? Is there any practice of courtship in the Bible? This chapter contains an exposition on courtship, which will empower you with a good understanding of the subject.

Definition of courtship

Courtship is defined as a relationship between a man and a woman who have agreed to get married. It is a relationship that is geared towards understanding each other and to determine whether the would-be couple are compatible for a successful marriage.

The period of courtship ranges from six months to three years or even longer in some cases. At the end of the courtship, if the couple believe they would make a successful marriage, a date is fixed for the marriage. The end of the courtship also marks the beginning of their engagement. If during or after the courtship, either or both the couple feel they are not compatible for marriage, the courtship is broken and the relationship terminated without ceremony.

Courtship and betrothal: are they the same?

Many people have mistaken betrothal for courtship. Let me quickly point out here that betrothal is not the same as courtship and there is no similarity between them. Betrothal, which also means espousal, can be defined as a marriage relationship in which a couple is required to live apart for a period of time after payment of the bride price.

The betrothal period can be for a year or even more. During this period, the bride is expected to use the bride price to trade and save money for her coming together with her husband. The groom on the other hand is expected, during the betrothal period, to build a home where he will live with his wife. It was during this betrothal period that Mary became pregnant after the Holy Spirit overshadowed her.

> *Now the birth of Jesus Christ was on this wise: When as his mother Mary was espoused to Joseph, before they came together, she was found with child of the Holy Ghost.*
>
> (Matthew 1:18)

During the betrothal period, the couple is regarded as husband and wife in as much as they are yet to live together. Another significant fact about betrothal is that unlike courtship, it can only be broken by divorce or by death.

> *Because Joseph her husband was a righteous man and did not want to expose her to public disgrace, he had in mind to divorce her quietly.*
>
> (Matthew 1:19 NIV)

From the above passage, we see the scripture referring to Joseph as Mary's husband during their betrothal period. This shows that betrothal is regarded as marriage. We also see Joseph planning to divorce Mary because he found out she was pregnant during the betrothal period. This also shows that just like marriage, only divorce or death can break up the relationship. In courtship, the man and woman are regarded as fiancé and fiancée and can break up the relationship at anytime, anyhow, with or without cause. Unlike betrothal, bride price is not paid in courtship. Betrothal and courtship are not the same.

How long should courtship last?

A courtship of three or five years is not enough for you to know if you are compatible with your intended spouse. This is because nobody behaves as his or her real self during courtship for fear of loosing the relationship. No matter how real you tend to be, there are always some reservations, especially when you don't want anything to break up the relationship.

Even when you feel that you or your spouse exhibited some true character during courtship, you will not be able to fully understand your spouse's character because the human character is never constant. **Human beings constantly change.** This is the reason why somebody close to you will tell you that he or she is surprised at a particular behaviour you put up. Because you have not exhibited such behaviour previously, the person becomes surprised at your action. Even mothers are sometimes surprised at some irregular behaviour put up by children who have lived with them all their lives.

You constantly change as you grow. Your character last year is different from your character this year, and your character next month will yet be different from your character today. Even your wisdom and understanding also increases as you study, and regresses when you no longer study. There is nothing constant in man. This means that 50 years of courtship is not enough to know if someone is compatible with you or not. Before you get used to a particular character, he or she would have put up a new one. No amount of years spent in courtship is enough to determine whether a couple is compatible for marriage. Apart from the fact that courtship cannot determine whether a couple is compatible, the length of courtship does not make a marriage successful.

Does courtship signify lack of trust in God?

Courtship signifies lack of trust in God. As a Christian who wants to get married, the first thing you should do is to pray for God's direction. In as much as you have the right of choice, it is better you allow your steps to be directed by God because He knows everything. He knows the end before the beginning.

God knows the spouse that is suitable for you. Rather than trying to use your own very limited knowledge to find your spouse, allow Him to direct you.

> *A man's heart deviseth his way: but the LORD directeth his steps.*
>
> (Proverbs 16:9)

You must never forget that it is always better to cast your cares on God. The Bible says,

> *Cast all your anxiety on him because he cares for you.*
>
> (1 Peter 5:7 NIV)

Once you pray for God's direction in your choice of spouse and He answers you, if the person is a true believer and you appreciate him or her, you don't need courtship anymore. God who knows the end before the beginning does not make mistakes. He has never made a mistake and will never make a mistake. You cannot be more intelligent than God. Even God's 'foolishness' is better than our wisdom.

> *For the foolishness of God is wiser than man's wisdom, and the weakness of God is stronger than man's strength.*
>
> (1 Corinthians 1:25 NIV)

If God directs your intended spouse to you, then it is a good match. When God answers your prayer by directing your intended spouse to you and you still want to go into courtship in order to use your own intelligence to know if you are compatible with the person, then you don't trust God.

In Isaac and Rebecca's marriage, we find a clear demonstration of trust and faith in God. From the start, Abraham's servant prayed to God.

> *And he said O LORD God of my master Abraham, I pray thee, send me good speed this day, and shew kindness unto my master Abraham.*
> *Behold, I stand here by the well of water; and the daughters of the men of the city come out to draw water:*
> *And let it come to pass, that the damsel to whom I shall say, Let down thy pitcher, I pray thee, that I may drink; and she shall*

say, Drink, and I will give thy camels drink also: let the same be she that thou hast appointed for thy servant Isaac; and thereby shall I know that thou hast shewed kindness unto my master.

(Genesis 24:12-14)

From the above passage, we see Eliezer, Abraham's servant doing the first thing anyone looking for a spouse should do – praying. It is also worthy of note that Eliezer did not only pray for direction, he also asked God to grant him speed.

And it came to pass, before he had done speaking, that, behold, Rebekah came out, who was born to Bethuel, son of Milcah, the wife of Nahor, Abraham's brother, with her pitcher upon her shoulder.
And the damsel was very fair to look upon, a virgin, neither had any man known her: and she went down to the well, and filled her pitcher, and came up.
And the servant ran to meet her, and said, Let me, I pray thee, drink a little water of thy pitcher.
And she said, Drink, my lord: and she hasted, and let down her pitcher upon her hand, and gave him drink.

*And when she had done giving him drink,
she said, I will draw water for thy camels
also, until they have done drinking.
And she hasted, and emptied her pitcher
into the trough, and ran again unto the
well to draw water, and drew for all his
camels.*

(Genesis 24:15-20)

In the passage above, first we see how God
granted Eliezer's prayer for speed by Rebekah
coming to the well even before he finished his
prayer. We also see how God answered Eliezer's
prayer for direction by Rebekah giving drink to
Eliezer and to all his camels. Eliezer realising
that God has answered his prayers, stopped his
search immediately. He did not attempt to meet
with another lady, and probably compare them
to see who was better, like most people would do
today. Because of his trust in God, he stopped
his search immediately.

*And it came to pass, as the camels had
done drinking, that the man took a golden
earring of half a shekel weight, and two
bracelets for her hands of ten shekels
weight of gold.*

(Genesis 24:22)

47

Eliezer giving Rebekah gold earrings and bracelets indicates his resolve to end his search and also his acceptance of Rebekah as Isaac's wife-to-be.

Later on, when Eliezer met with Rebekah's family, he told them how Abraham had asked him to get a wife for Isaac from among his people. He also told them how he prayed to God by the well.

Behold, I stand by the well of water; and it shall come to pass, that when the virgin cometh forth to draw water, and I say to her, Give me, I pray thee, a little water of thy pitcher to drink;

And she say to me, Both drink thou, and I will also draw for thy camels: let the same be the woman whom the LORD hath appointed out for my master's son.

And before I had done speaking in mine heart, behold, Rebekah came forth with her pitcher on her shoulder; and she went down unto the well, and drew water: and I said unto her, Let me drink, I pray thee.

And she made haste, and let down her pitcher from her shoulder, and said, Drink, and I will give thy camels drink also: so I drank, and she made the camels drink also.

(Genesis 24:43-46)

After Eliezer told Rebekah's family how he had prayed to God and how God answered his prayer by Rebekah coming forth, they believed him. Because they believed that if God had directed Rebekah to Eliezer that every thing is in order since God cannot make a mistake, they granted Eliezer the permission to take Rebekah to her spouse.

Then Laban and Bethuel answered and said, The thing proceedeth from the LORD: we cannot speak unto thee bad or good.
Behold, Rebekah is before thee, take her, and go, and let her be thy master's son's wife, as the LORD hath spoken.

(Genesis 24: 50-51)

So, Laban and Bethuel granted Eliezer permission to take Rebekah to her spouse. It is also important to note that it is for this same reason that Isaac married Rebekah even without seeing her face.

For she had said unto the servant, What man is this that walketh in the field to meet us? And the servant had said, It is my master: therefore she took a veil, and covered herself.
And the servant told Isaac all things that he had done.
And Isaac brought her into his mother Sarah's tent, and took Rebekah, and she became his wife; and he loved her: and Isaac was comforted after his mother's death.

(Genesis 24:65-67)

In verse 65, she covered her face with a veil in accordance with their custom that the groom had no knowledge of her before their marriage. In verse 66, Eliezer told Isaac everything that happened including how he prayed and how God answered his prayer. Just like Laban and Bethuel told Abraham's servant that because it is from the Lord they could not oppose it, Isaac trusted in God and married her immediately, even without seeing her face.

Isaac married Rebekah without courtship because he had trust and faith in God. Beloved, this is faith. Their marriage was highly successful by all standards. The reason is that God had seen the success of their marriage even before answering the servant's prayer by directing Rebekah to him. **The good news is that God is still God. He has not changed and will never change. The same way He directed Rebekah to Eliezer is the same way he answers anyone who prays for direction.**

The devil is very subtle. He injects into the minds of people thoughts that the biblical principles of marriage are outdated, and as such should not be practised in this new age. This is not true because God's Word does not change. His Word is life every day and can never be outdated. God and His Word are one and do not change. God is the same yesterday, today and forever. The marriage institution, which was ordained by God, is also as constant as God. The marriage institution never changes. It is constant. Couples though may change, but the marriage institution never changes. No matter the number of separations or divorces, the marriage institution remains the same. **So if God, His Word, and the marriage institution are constant, then it means that the steps taken in the scripture to find a spouse can also be used today and forever.**

If God directs your steps to your intended spouse, you do not need to go into courtship to ascertain if the person is compatible with you. God who knows every thing knows the best for you. All you should be concerned with is whether you like the person and whether he or she is a true believer.

Is courtship for Christians?

The answer is NO. The word courtship is not in the Bible. From the book of Genesis to the book of Revelation, there is no mention of courtship. Neither is there any relationship in the Bible that looks like or is similar to courtship. In the second book of Timothy, chapter 3, verse 16, the scripture cautions Christians against the use of doctrines that are not in the Bible.

All scripture is given by inspiration of God, and is profitable for doctrine, for reproof, for correction, for instruction in righteousness.

(2 Timothy 3:16)

For every relationship approved in the kingdom of God, there are guidelines stated in the Bible for such relationships. The Bible is flawless – there is nothing left out.

Every word of God is flawless; he is a shield to those who take refuge in him. Do not add to his words, or he will rebuke you and prove you a liar.
(Proverbs 30:5-6 NIV)

Any doctrine not found in the Bible is not a mistake; it means it is not for us. There is no courtship relationship in the Bible and there are no guidelines for such relationship. Every doctrine that we ought to practise is in the Bible. For instance, the guidelines for husband-wife relationship can be seen in the book of Ephesians.

Wives submit yourselves unto your own husband, as unto the Lord.
(Ephesians 5:22)

Husbands, love your wives even as Christ also loved the church and gave himself for it.
(Ephesians 5:25)

In the next chapter of the same book of Ephesians, you will see guidelines for parents-children relationship.

Children, obey your parents in the Lord:
for this is right.
Honour thy father and mother; which is
the first commandment with promise;
That it may be well with thee, and thou
mayest live long on the earth.

(Ephesians 6:1-3)

And, ye fathers, provoke not your children
to wrath: but bring them up in the nurture
and admonition of the Lord.

(Ephesians 6:4)

In the same chapter, you will also find guidelines on how servants are to relate with their masters.

Servants, be obedient to them that are
your masters according to the flesh, with
fear and trembling, in singleness of your
heart, as unto Christ;
Not with eyeservice, as menpleasers; but
as the servants of Christ, doing the will of
God from the heart;
With good will doing service, as to the
Lord, and not to men:
Knowing that whatsoever good thing any
man doeth, the same shall he receive of

the Lord, whether he be bond or free.
(Ephesians 6:5-8)

Masters are also told how to relate with their servants.

And, ye masters, do the same things unto them, forbearing threatening: knowing that your Master also is in heaven; neither is there respect of persons with him.
(Ephesians 6:9)

For every relationship that is recognised in the kingdom of God, there are specific guidelines. The relationship termed courtship is not mentioned in the Bible and there are no guidelines in the Bible for such relationship. Courtship is not for believers. If courtship were for true believers, Mary the mother of our Lord and Master Jesus Christ would have gone through courtship before marrying Joseph. Courtship is not in the scriptures and it is a device of the devil.

Once God directs you to a true believer who you appreciate, have faith, trust in God and marry the person. Going into courtship is not only a display of lack of trust in God; but you will never know your spouse well enough because as human beings, we constantly change. I married my wife without courtship because I appreciate her and I was sure God directed her to me. Today, we are enjoying our marriage tremendously.

There is no practice of courtship in the Bible. The Bible is complete and perfect. There is no mistake and there is no omission in the scripture. Courtship is not a biblical doctrine.

History of courtship

If courtship is not a biblical doctrine, then how did it start? The first record of courtship was in 1708. The courtship was between Samuel Gerish, a Boston bookseller, and Mary Sewall, the daughter of Puritan magistrate, Samuel Sewall. After Samuel Gerish had indicated his interest in Mary, Judge Sewall did some investigations on Samuel Gerish and found out he had dated three other girls in the past and dropped them. In order to protect his daughter, Judge Sewall wrote a lengthy letter to Samuel Gerish's father asking him to state the kind of relationship his son wanted with Mary. Samuel Gerish's father replied the letter explaining that his son wanted to marry Mary. On receipt of the letter, Judge Sewall then permitted the relationship and stated the conditions of the courtship. Their courtship lasted for six months and they got married.

Another account of courtship was recorded one hundred and thirty years later, in 1838. The courtship was between Theodore Dwight Weld and Angelina Grimke, the daughter of a rich South Carolina slave trader who had turned against slavery. Theodore had written a letter to Angelina stating "that for a long time you have had my whole heart." He also stated that he had "no expectation and almost no hope that [his] feelings are in any degree reciprocated by you." He asked her to express her feelings. Angelina replied the letter stating "I feel, my Theodore, that we are the two halves of one whole, a twain one, two bodies animated by one soul and that the Lord has given us to each other."

Afterwards Theodore wrote another letter telling her he didn't deserve her love because he was not well educated, was impatient, and careless in appearance. Angelina replied, telling him her weaknesses as well: pride, high temperament, and that she was in a relationship before. Afterwards, they got married.

Please take note that in 1708, when Samuel Gerish and Mary Sewall courted, there was much parental involvement in marriages. This parental involvement declined drastically by

1838 when Theodore Weld and Angelina Grimke had their courtship. In the Samuel and Mary courtship, their parents wrote letters. But in the Theodore and Angelina courtship, they wrote their letters themselves. Children started to choose their spouse without parental influence and interference. Courtship became freer and marriage itself became more difficult, especially for ladies. Besides courtship becoming more of a testing period for the ladies, many ladies were being used and dumped by men. Marriage became more difficult and many ladies at that time opted never to marry at all.

Apart from the fact that courtship made marriage difficult, unbelievers originated it. It has nothing to do with Christianity. It is not a biblical doctrine. As Christians, we are allowed to practise only biblical doctrines. Instead of using your own wisdom to choose your spouse, allow God to direct your spouse to you. Once God directs your spouse to you, there is no need to go into courtship to find out if you are compatible. God, who does not make mistakes, knows who is most suitable for you. All you need to do is to get married trusting God and you will surely have a successful and enjoyable marriage.

Courtship: a device of the devil?

The devil has made people to rely on their rational or human sense of judgement instead of seeking God's counsel. Courtship relies on human reasoning; it is a device of the devil. In man's wisdom, entering into courtship is the best way to choose one's right spouse.

In other subjects like prosperity, healing, holiness, and many others, we follow the scripture accordingly, but when it comes to the issue of marriage, especially finding a spouse, we tend to be rational rather than follow the scripture. On the subject of prosperity for instance, the church has been able to teach Christians to know their rights. We pay tithe amongst other things in order to prosper and secure our wealth.

Abraham paid the first tithe to Mechezedek over 4,000 years ago. Initially, the church saw it as outdated and there was no prosperity in the kingdom. But as soon as we got the revelation that God's Word is alive forever, we started paying tithe and prosperity came into the church. Paying tithe is not rational in the sense that if you use your human sense of reasoning, you will never pay it.

We are in the world but not of the world. We don't do things like people of the world. For instance, while the people of the world say that 'seeing is believing', in the kingdom of God, it is 'believing is seeing'. Paying of tithe is something unbelievers have not been able to understand. Christians simply pay tithe because it is God's Word. In as much as it was done thousands of years ago, it is still working very well!

God's Word is forever. Finding your spouse as it was done in the scripture is not outdated. You can never understand marriage or go into marriage with human sense of reasoning because it is a mystery. The Word of God says it is a mystery.

> *For this cause shall a man leave his father and mother, and shall be joined unto his wife, and they two shall be one flesh.*
> *This is a great mystery: but I speak concerning Christ and the church.*
> *Nevertheless let every one of you in particular so love his wife even as himself; and the wife see that she reverence her husband.*
>
> (Ephesians 5:31-33)

For every principle of God, we are expected to use the doctrines in the scripture and not our human sense of reasoning. If you pray like

Eliezer prayed, and God directs your intended spouse to you, you don't need to go into courtship because God knows what you need better than you do. If you appreciate the person and he or she is a true believer, then marry him or her.

The ills of courtship

Courtship has caused many Christians, especially ladies, to be broken hearted and frustrated. It has also led to late marriages, separations and divorces. Some have even backslid from the faith because of courtship.

During courtship, it is difficult to avoid sleeping with each other. If you don't see regularly, the initial aim, which is to understand each other, will be defeated. On the other hand, when you see regularly, the tendency that you will fall into the sin of fornication is very high. When that happens, the man in most cases looses trust in the lady, thinking she may be sleeping with other men as well. This lack of trust often leads to the breaking of their courtship. When the relationship is broken, the lady becomes broken hearted and frustrated. In extreme cases, the lady will hate and distrust all men; even when she eventually gets married, she may never trust her husband.

Some ladies backslide from Christianity after their courtship is broken, especially when the man that broke the courtship is a dedicated worker or a leader in her church. The lady looses confidence in the Church and may never attend services again, not even in other churches. The terrible thing about falling into the sin of fornication is that even in cases where the man and the woman really appreciate each other, they can still break up after fornicating. If such couple never got involved in courtship and had married after God directed their steps to meet, they would have had sex legally and lived happily as husband and wife. The truth is that God cannot order the steps of a wrong spouse to you.

After courtship, the couple believing they are perfect match go into marriage committing themselves to each other. The period of courtship makes them feel they have been tested and proven to be a perfect match. This notion of being a perfect match will make them expect perfect behaviour from one another and unknowingly depend on each other for happiness. After a while when one of the couple makes a mistake and puts up an irregular character, the other feels betrayed. This is bound to happen because no human being is perfect. Because of the notion of 'perfection' developed during courtship, the other is so surprised and disappointed. In some cases, it leads to separation or divorce. This is how courtship leads to many broken marriages.

Any couple that depends on each other, rather than on God, for their happiness will always be disappointed because no one is perfect. The major adverse effect that courtship has on couples is that it makes them commit themselves to one another, thereby depending on each other for happiness. When either of the couple is not getting the required happiness, disappointment and a feeling of insecurity sets in. If care is not taken, it may lead to separation or divorce. Thus, courtship, which many view as a tool of making marriages successful, actually leads to broken marriages. If courtship does not make a marriage successful, what then determines a successful marriage? In the next chapter, I will show you what makes a marriage successful.

CHAPTER FOUR

What Makes a Marriage Successful?

*W*hat makes a marriage successful is your dependence on God rather than on your spouse for happiness, and your willingness to work out your marriage on a daily basis until death.

> *For all have sinned, and come short of the glory of God.*
>
> (Romans 3:23)

You must realise that no one is perfect. There is no perfect husband or wife. We are all bound to make mistakes. There is no perfect spouse on earth. Because your spouse is imperfect, you must never rely on him or her for your happiness in marriage. If you rely on your spouse for happiness, you will be disappointed. Your spouse being imperfect would always fail you; and when that happens, you will be disappointed. The disappointment may lead to frustration and if care is not taken, it may lead to separation and divorce.

For you to enjoy your marriage, you must never rely on your spouse for happiness. **Your spouse does not have the ability to provide your happiness.**

Stop trusting in man, who has but a breath in his nostrils. Of what account is he?
> (Isaiah 2:22 NIV)

The Bible passage above warns against relying on a human being whom it describes as *who has only a breath in his nostrils*. No person including your spouse can provide you happiness. You must rely on God for your happiness in marriage. Besides being the owner of the marriage institution, He is also perfect and can never disappoint you.

Those who trust in the LORD are like Mount Zion, which cannot be shaken but endures forever.
> (Psalm 125:1 NIV)

For true happiness in marriage, you must rely on God rather than on your spouse.

Having known that your spouse is imperfect and bound to make mistakes, you will no longer be disappointed when he or she offends you. Rather than being disappointed in your spouse's wrong doing, you should see it as an area of weakness in him or her and offer a hand of love to your spouse in that area of weakness. If your spouse does something wrong to you, rather than quarrelling or keeping malice with him or her, you should realise that he or she did it because of his or her weakness in that area. What you need to do at that time is to offer a hand of love, by forgiving and correcting in love. By doing so, you are working out your marriage. **For you to effectively work out your marriage, you must make sacrifices for your spouse even when he or she does not deserve it.** You must practise true love.

Please note that it is only in working out your marriage on a daily basis that you can enjoy it. **The moment you stop working out your marriage, it will start collapsing**. It is a lifetime work. **Marriage is a school you can never graduate from**. There is no short cut to enjoying your marriage. You must work it out to have a successful marriage. The importance of working out one's marriage for a lifetime is symbolised in the ancient Jewish marriage ceremony.

After blessing the couple in a marriage ceremony, the Rabbi conducting the marriage wraps a wineglass with a napkin, and the groom holding the bride shatters it.

The shattering of the wineglass symbolises the destruction of the temple. Each piece of the broken glass represents one of various experiences and trials that will come in the marriage. The couple will now be charged with the responsibility of rebuilding the glass symbolically, until all the pieces of the glass are put together.

To emphasise the importance of working out their marriage throughout their lives, the Rabbi takes two of the broken pieces. He throws one into a river and the other, he takes home. This means that the couple will never be able to put all the pieces together. The essence is to make the couple realise they are not perfect and the need to work out their marriage until death.

By working out your marriage daily, you will not only have peace and unity in your marriage, you will also have a successful and enjoyable marriage.

CHAPTER FIVE

Can God Choose a Spouse for me?

efore I proceed to show you the scriptural conditions for the choice of one's spouse, let me first clarify whose duty it is to choose a spouse. Many people feel that God can choose a spouse for them or reveal to them whom to marry. God does not choose a wife for any man and God does not tell any man whom to marry. In fact, God **cannot** choose a wife for any man. I have also heard many people say that because Adam accused God that it was the woman He gave him that led him to sin, God stopped choosing wives for men. This assumption is not true, as God did not choose Eve for Adam.

Eve wasn't the first and only creature God presented to Adam. There were other creatures, but his choice was Eve. Adam chose Eve himself. Man is a free moral agent. We are the only creatures of God that are free moral agents because we were created in the image and likeness of God. God does not and will not interfere with our right of choice. Let us take a little excursion into the scripture to see how Adam made his choice of Eve.

And the LORD God said, It is not good that the man should be alone; I will make an help meet for him.

And out of the ground the LORD God formed every beast of the field, and every fowl of the air; and brought them unto Adam to see what he would call them: and whatsoever Adam called every living creature, that was the name thereof.

And Adam gave names to all cattle, and to the fowl of the air, and to every beast of the field; but for Adam there was not found an help meet for him.

And the LORD God caused a deep sleep to fall upon Adam, and he slept: and he took one of his ribs, and closed up the flesh instead thereof;

And the rib, which the LORD God had taken from man, made him a woman, and

brought her unto the man.
And Adam said, This is now bone of my
bones, and flesh of my flesh: she shall be
called Woman, because she was taken out
of man.
Therefore shall a man leave his father
and his mother, and shall cleave unto his
wife: and they shall be one flesh.

(Genesis 2:18-24)

In verse 18 of Genesis chapter 2, God established the fact that man should not be alone. He
also decided to make a *help meet* for man. In
verse 19, He went on to make the *help meet*. It is
important to note in this verse that God's primary aim of bringing the beasts of the field and
fowls of the air to Adam is not for the purpose of
naming. Many people mistake it to be a naming
ceremony. The Bible says,

And out of the ground the LORD God
formed every beast of the field, and
every fowl of the air; and brought them
unto Adam to see what he would call
them: and whatsoever Adam called
every living creature, that was the name
thereof.

(Genesis 2:19)

Please note here that God brought them unto Adam to see what he would call them and not for Adam to name them. They have two different meanings. If it were a naming ceremony, the Bible would have said God brought them unto Adam to be named. But in this case, God wanted to see what Adam would call them, because whatever name he would call any of them would determine his choice. In this verse, the Bible is saying that in searching for a *help meet*, whatever name Adam called the beast of the field and the fowls of the air would become their name thereafter.

May I also state here that if it were a naming ceremony, God would have brought all his creatures, including every creature that live in the water because He could do so. But because it was a search for a suitable mate for Adam and not a naming ceremony, God brought only the creatures that could live on land. In verse 20, Adam gave names to all the cattle, fowls of the air, and to every beast, but did not find any *helpmeet* of his choice among the creatures. That is the reason he didn't choose any of them for his *helpmeet*.

In the same verse 20, the scripture says *but for Adam there was not found an help meet for him*. This means there was a search among the beasts of the field and fowls of the air but no suitable mate was found for him. The word 'found' indicates that there was a search. Because Adam didn't choose from any of the creatures formed out of the ground, God then formed woman out of Adam and brought her to him.

Note well that the same way God brought the beasts of the field and the fowls of the air to Adam to see what he would call them, so He also formed and brought the woman to Adam to see what he would call her.

> *And the rib, which the LORD God had taken from man, made he a woman, and brought her unto the man.*
>
> (Genesis 2:22)

This verse also confirms that the purpose of bringing the beasts of the field and fowls of the air to Adam was the same as bringing Eve to Adam. The purpose was undoubtedly for him to choose a *help meet*.

Another spectacular thing happened in verse 23. When Adam saw the woman, he exclaimed: *This is now bone of my bones and flesh of my flesh*. The '<u>now</u>' in Adam's statement clearly indicates that none of the creatures previously brought to him was acceptable to him. It meant that he had finally found an acceptable mate, so he declared: *She shall be called Woman, because she was taken out of Man.* Please note that in this same verse, Adam also gave a name to the woman just as he had given names to the beasts of the field and the fowls of the air.

So, their marriage took place immediately because the search for a *help meet* was over.

> *Therefore shall a man leave his father and his mother, and shall cleave unto his wife: and they shall be one flesh.*
>
> (Genesis 2:24)

What I want you to understand here is that God did not force Adam to marry Eve. Adam had other choices but preferred Eve. God has never and will never choose a wife for any man. God does not interfere with our right of choice. It is your responsibility to choose your spouse. What God did was to bring the woman (Eve) to Adam and allowed him to make his choice.

God can order your steps to meet with your future spouse.

> *The steps of a good man are ordered by the LORD...*
>
> (Psalm 37:23)

This is one reason why you should not take for granted the people that cross your path each day. God can direct your spouse to you but He will not choose for you, and will not force you to marry the person. **The choice is yours to make.**

CHAPTER SIX

How to Choose Your Spouse

*T*here are principles in the scripture that guide us in the choice of spouse. In this chapter, I will illustrate the most fundamental of these principles.

Major condition of choosing your spouse

The principal step in the choice of one's spouse is to confirm that he or she is a believer. You must marry from the family of believers.

> *And Abraham said unto his eldest servant of his house, that ruled over all that he had, Put, I pray thee, thy hand under my thigh:*
> *And I will make thee swear by the LORD, the God of heaven, and the God of the*

earth, that thou shalt not take a wife unto my son of the daughters of the Canaanites, among whom I dwell:
But thou shalt go unto my country, and to my kindred, and take a wife unto my son Isaac.

(Genesis 24:2-4)

Here, Abraham requests his servant to get a wife for his son Isaac. He then goes on to specifically instruct the servant to get a wife from among his kindred. The gravity of this condition is demonstrated by the fact that Abraham asked his servant to swear an oath that he must get a wife for Isaac from among his (Abraham's) family. If it weren't so important, Abraham wouldn't have asked his servant to swear an oath.

Every believer is part of the family or kindred of Abraham because we are children of Abraham.

Know you therefore that they which are of faith, the same are the children of Abraham.

(Galatians 3:7)

Since the family of believers are the children of Abraham, then we are of the family of

Abraham. If our father Abraham made his servant to swear an oath that he will get a wife for Isaac from among his family, then it is important that we should marry from among the family of believers. You must marry from the family of believers. Marriage to a person outside the kingdom of God is unacceptable.

The scripture explains this further.

Do not be yoked together with unbelievers. For what do righteousness and wickedness have in common? Or what fellowship can light have with darkness? What harmony is there between Christ and Belial? What does a believer have in common with an unbeliever?

What agreement is there between the temple of God and idols? For we are the temple of the living God. As God has said: "I will live with them and walk among them, and I will be their God, and they will be my people."

(2 Corinthians 6:14-16 NIV)

The New Testament passage above clearly condemns marriage between a believer and an unbeliever. Intermarriages or marriages with unbelievers are not entertained in the kingdom of

God. In fact, there is a punishment for any inter-marriage.

> *Neither shalt thou make marriages with them; thy daughter thou shalt not give unto his son, nor his daughter shalt thou take unto thy son.*
> *For they will turn away thy son from following me, that they may serve other gods: so will the anger of the LORD be kindled against you,' and destroy thee suddenly.*

(Deuteronomy 7:3-4)

If both of you are true believers, then the same marriage manual, the Holy Bible, would guide your marriage. Because one marriage manual is acceptable to both of you, it makes the union easy. You must never marry an unbeliever. Your choice of spouse must be from the family of believers.

How do I know a true believer?

The first step in knowing who is a true believer is that you must ensure you are a true Christian. You must have a personal relationship with Jesus Christ before you can know who is a true believer. When you have a relationship with Jesus Christ, the Holy Spirit will live in you. It is only when the Spirit of God lives in you that He can reveal to you who is a true Christian.

> *...And it is the Spirit that beareth witness, because the Spirit is truth.*
>
> (1 John 5:6)

By reason of the Spirit of God in you, when you meet a true believer, the Spirit will bear witness to your spirit to know there is the Spirit of God in that person.

> *Deep calleth unto deep...*
>
> (Psalm 42:7)

That a person attends church services or is a worker in a church is not enough reason to conclude that he or she is a true believer. Though they may be good reasons, but certainly not the best way of determining who is a true Christian. You must allow the Spirit of God to guide you in knowing who is a true believer.

CHAPTER SEVEN

Seeking God's Direction

I have heard some people ignorantly say that Christians do not need to seek the direction and guidance of God on whom to marry because the right of choice is theirs. I would like to state here that in as much as the right of choice is yours, you must never marry without God's direction or guidance.

Why seek for God's direction?

Because of the importance of marriage, you must never go into it without God's guidance. In as much as the right of choice of spouse is yours, you must aspire to do the will of God at all times. In an issue as marriage which is the most fundamental institution created by God, you must seek God's guidance concerning your spouse.

God who knows the end before the beginning can never make a mistake, and as such, knows who is most suitable for you.

Because the foolishness of God is wiser than men; and the weakness of God is stronger than men.

(1 Corinthians 1:25)

You must seek God's direction before choosing a spouse. **If you, a Christian, marry without the direction of God, then how different are you from unbelievers?** If God is Lord over your life, you must never do anything without Him. You must never go into marriage without His guidance. Some people confess Christ with their mouths but their actions say that God does not exist.

They profess that they know God; but in works they deny him, being abominable and disobedient, and unto every good work reprobate.

(Titus 1:16)

So, we should be Christians both in our confession and in our action. If you realise you have a heavenly father who knows every thing, the best would be to seek his guidance in everything you do, especially in an important issue as marriage.

When you go into marriage without God's guidance, you are like a person that picks a lucky dip. In a lucky dip, you don't know what you will pick-up until you have picked it. It may be what you want or it may not be. So is anyone who marries without the guidance of God. The person may marry the right spouse or the wrong one. If you want to be sure of marrying the right spouse, ask God to guide you.

Seeking God's direction also means trusting in God absolutely. You should entrust Him with your worries and concerns. The Bible says: *Cast all your anxiety on him because he cares for you.* (1 peter 5:7 NIV)

How to seek God's direction

To have God's guidance and direction in choosing a spouse, you must ask Him in prayer. Marriage is so important to God that He answers every marriage prayer that is in accordance with His Word. If you also ask God to grant you speed in directing your intended spouse to you, He will answer you immediately. Eliezer, Abraham's servant, while praying for God's direction for Isaac's spouse, asked God to grant him speed and God answered both prayers immediately. God directed Rebekah to him straightaway. *as far as its in line with his word.*

> And he said O LORD God of my master Abraham, I pray thee, send me good speed this day, and shew kindness unto my master Abraham.
> Behold, I stand here by the well of water; and the daughters of the men of the city come out to draw water:
> And let it come to pass, that the damsel to whom I shall say, Let down thy pitcher, I pray thee, that I may drink; and she shall say, Drink, and I will give thy camels drink also: let the same be she that thou hast appointed for thy servant Isaac; and thereby shall I know that thou hast shewed kindness unto my master.
> And it came to pass, before he had done speaking, that, behold, Rebekah came out, who was born to Bethuel, son of Milcah, the wife of Nahor, Abraham's brother, with her pitcher upon her shoulder.
>
> (Genesis 24:12-15)

Here the Bible records that before Abraham's

servant concluded his prayer for God's guidance in choosing a spouse for Isaac, Rebekah came forth. The truth is that it is more important to God that you get married than it is to you. God desires that every adult Christian should be married.

Because of the importance of marriage to God, He motivates people to marry. The scripture says,

> *Whoso findeth a wife findeth a good thing, and obtaineth favour of the LORD.*
> (Proverbs 18:22)

The motivation God gives to any person that gets married is favour. If God promises you the gift of favour to motivate you to get married, then He will not relent in answering your prayer for guidance in choosing your spouse. If you have not found a spouse yet, begin to ask God now for guidance, and the same God who answered the prayer of Abraham's servant will answer yours, in the mighty name of Jesus Christ our saviour. Amen.

How do I know whom God has directed to me?

The first and basic way of knowing if God has directed a particular person to you is to ascertain whether the person is a true believer. God cannot direct an unbeliever to you because the scripture does not support intermarriages between believers and unbelievers. None of God's action is contrary to His Word.

> *Neither shalt thou make marriages with them; thy daughter thou shalt not give unto his son, nor his daughter shalt thou take unto thy son.*
> *For they will turn away thy son from following me, that they may serve other gods: so will the anger of the LORD be kindled against you, and destroy thee suddenly.*
>
> (Deuteronomy 7:3-4)

From the above passage, you will observe that God's Word does not only say you should not marry an unbeliever but there is also a punishment for anyone who does it. God cannot order your steps to marry an unbeliever contrary to His Word. God respects His Word even above His name and cannot break His Word.

Another important way of knowing the person God has directed to you is being at peace in your heart.

Great peace have they who love your law,
and nothing can make them stumble.
                              (Psalm 119:165 NIV)

In deciding to marry the person God has ordered your steps to meet, you will have peace in your heart. If God has not ordered your steps to meet with the person, the Spirit of God in you will be in disagreement with your decision to marry the person, and you will not have peace in your heart.

I must warn that dreams are not very reliable in knowing whom God has directed to you because God is not the only source of dreams. Dreams can come from the devil and can also come from one's own thoughts. Because of the various sources of dreams, many people find it difficult to interpret their dreams correctly. This makes dreams unreliable in knowing whom God has directed to you.

Once your decision to marry a person is in line with the will of God, the Spirit of God in you will be in agreement with your own spirit, and that will in turn produce peace in your heart. This still remains the best way of knowing whom God has directed to you for marriage.

CHAPTER EIGHT

Fornication

*F*ornication is one of the biggest obstacles in the choice of one's right spouse. It has both direct and indirect effect on one's choice of spouse. What exactly is fornication?

What is fornication?

Fornication comes from a Greek word, *porneia*. *Porneia*, according to *The New Strong's Exhaustive Concordance of the Bible*, literally means harlotry, adultery, incest, and every type of unlawful sex. Based on this understanding, fornication can be defined as an unlawful sexual sin including sex between unmarried persons, lesbianism, homosexuality, masturbation, incest, adultery, and every form of sexual sin.

For a clearer illustration, let us look at two

different translations of a particular verse of the Bible that makes reference to fornication, the King James Version (KJV) and the New International Version (NIV).

> *Flee fornication. Every sin a man doeth is without the body; but he that committeth fornication sinneth against his own body.*
> (1Corinthians 6:18)

> *Flee from sexual immorality. All other sins a man commits are outside his body, but he who sins sexually sins against his own body.*
> (1Corinthians 6:18 NIV)

The passages above are saying the same thing. The difference is only in their choice of words. While King James Version of the Bible calls it fornication, the New International Version calls it sexual immorality. They are both correct. Fornication is any type of sexual immorality.

How does fornication affect the choice of right spouse?

> *What? Know ye not that he which is joined to an harlot is one body? for two,*

saith he, shall be one flesh.
                    (1Corinthians 6:16)

Sex is a covenant between the persons involved. When two persons fornicate, they become one flesh; they automatically enter into a blood covenant without knowing it. Such blood covenant causes an undue obsession to develop in either the man, the lady, or in both. Such obsession has the power to make the persons go into marriage without putting into consideration the biblical principles of choosing a right spouse.

Flee from sexual immorality. All other sins a man commits are outside his body, but he who sins sexually sins against his own body.
Do you not know that your body is a temple of the Holy Spirit, who is in you, whom you have received from God? You are not your own;
You were bought at a price. Therefore honor God with your body.
                    (1 Corinthians 6:18-20 NIV)

The body of every believer is a temple of the Holy Spirit. Whenever a believer indulges in any form of sexual immorality, the Spirit of God departs from the person. It is the worst thing that can happen to any believer. No wonder David during his confession and prayer after fornicating with Bath-sheba pleaded with God not to take away the Holy Spirit from him.

> *Cast me not away from thy presence; and take not thy holy spirit from me.*
>
> (Psalm 51:11)

Fornication causes the Holy Spirit to depart from a believer, and when that happens, the Spirit can no longer bear witness to the believer. It is the Spirit of God in a believer that can only confirm to him or her if an intended spouse is a true believer. It is also the presence of the Spirit of God in a believer that will confirm whether his or her meeting with an intended spouse was ordered by God. In a situation where the Spirit of God departs from a believer, he or she is headed for a wrong choice.

When a person gets involved in any form of sexual immorality, the devil has a legal reason to attack such person. The devil has no power over a Christian; but when a Christian commits a sexual sin, he or she becomes open to the attack of the enemy. A legal doorway is thus established for the devil to attack such person. The Bible speaking in the book of Ecclesiastes says,

> *He that diggeth a pit shall fall into it; and*
> *whoso breaketh an hedge, a serpent shall*
> *bite him.*
>
> (Ecclesiastes 10:8)

This legal attack by the devil has the capacity of causing, among other things, delayed marriages.

Causes of fornication

Fornication like most sins starts when the devil injects thoughts into the minds of people. The thoughts can come into the person as his or her own thoughts. A person may, for instance, find himself/herself thinking of how he/she needs to indulge in a particular type of sexual sin.

> *But I fear, lest by any means, as the ser-*
> *pent beguiled Eve through subtlety, so*
> *your minds should be corrupted from the*
> *simplicity that is in Christ.*
>
> (2 Corinthians 11:3)

When the devil injects thoughts of fornication into a believer and the person accepts it, he or she will end up fornicating. Once a believer commits fornication, the Holy Spirit will depart from the person. Apart from the Holy Spirit departing from the person, any demon possessing the other party that he or she commits fornication with will immediately take possession of him or her.

> *What? Know ye not that he which is joined to an harlot is one body? for two, saith he, shall be one flesh.*
> (1 Corinthians 6:16)

Any two that commits fornication become one flesh, and every demon in one will possess the other. Because the demons live in the person, they take control of the person's mind and he or she will no longer be able to resist the temptation of sex.

Not only will the demons make the person commit fornication anytime they want sex, the person will also be committing only the type of sexual sins the demons want. The person will no longer have control over his or her mind. This is the reason why many fornicators can't explain what makes them commit sexual sins.

Thank God, fornication can be checked and stopped completely.

How to stop fornication

The first thing to do if you have ever indulged in any form of sexual immorality is to confess to God and ask Him for forgiveness from the depth of your heart. He is just and merciful, and will forgive you.

> *If we confess our sins, he is faithful and just to forgive us our sins, and to cleanse us from all unrighteousness.*
>
> (1 John 1:9)

After the confession, the next step is to cast away every contrary spirit that may be operating in your life because of the sexual sins you committed. Command them never to come back again. Please note that it is important to cast away every contrary spirit from your life. **If there is the presence of any contrary spirit in your life, you cannot control your mind whenever the devil injects thoughts of fornication into you.**

Ask God to close every doorway that may have been opened in your life due to any sexual sin. The closing of spiritual doorways in your life is necessary to ensure no other contrary spirits can have access to you.

The confession and prayer will help you gain control of your mind and stop the fornication. This however, does not exempt you from further temptations of fornication. The only advantage you have is that you will gain control of your mind. If there will be further temptations to fornicate, how then can fornication be completely avoided?

How to avoid fornication completely

Considering the fact that the major cause of fornication is by the devil injecting thoughts of fornication into the minds of people, it is important to be able to know when the devil is injecting such thoughts into your mind.

There are three sources of thoughts in a believer's mind: thoughts from the Holy Spirit, thoughts from the devil and the person's own thoughts. There is the need to crosscheck and identify who is responsible for every thought that comes into your mind before accepting it. The only way you can do this is by verifying every thought to see if they are in obedience to the lordship of Jesus Christ.

Casting down imaginations, and every high thing that exalteth itself against the knowledge of God, and bringing into captivity every thought to the obedience of Christ.

(2 Corinthians 10:5)

Once you realise that the thought coming into your mind is not in obedience to the lordship of Jesus Christ, you must do what Jesus Christ did when the devil tempted him. Jesus said to him: *Away from me, Satan* (Matthew 4:10 NIV). Whenever thoughts of fornication come into your mind, resist the devil, command him to flee and he will flee from you. Open your mouth and command the devil to flee from you. Jesus did it and the devil fled from him.

Submit yourselves therefore to God. Resist the devil, and he will flee from you.

(James 4:7)

Apart from resisting the devil, you must constantly renew your mind with the Word of God. This is the only way you can ensure being in control of your mind. God's desire is that every Christian should have control of his or her mind. To achieve this, you must constantly renew your mind with the Word of God.

> *And be not conformed to this world: but be ye transformed by the renewing of your mind, that ye may prove what is that good, and acceptable, and perfect, will of God.*
>
> (Romans 12:2)

To renew your mind, you must study and listen to the Word of God always.

The third way to avoid fornication is to avoid sleeping in the same apartment and staying in dark places with your intended spouse. The Bible admonishes us to *abstain from all appearance of evil* (1 Thessalonians 5:22). You must avoid being alone with any person you may likely commit sexual sin with.

Finally, ask God continually and continuously to give you the grace to overcome the temptation of fornication.

> *And lead us not into temptation, but deliver us from evil: For thine is the kingdom, and the power, and the glory, for ever. Amen.*
>
> (Matthew 6:13)

Take the right stand now! And do not get involved in any sexual sin anymore.

CHAPTER NINE

Some Vital Marital Issues

*I*n this chapter, I have used the biblical principles of marriage to explain some vital issues that affect the choice of spouse.

What is matchmaking?

Matchmaking can be defined as an introduction of a man and a woman to each other with the intention of marriage. The first match-made marriage recorded in the Bible is the Isaac and Rebecca marriage arranged by Eliezer, Abraham's servant. Eliezer can be regarded as the first matchmaker recorded in the Bible. Since then matchmaking has continued even unto this generation.

Is it good to marry through matchmaking?

A lot of criticisms have been levelled against matchmaking. Though many marriages in the Bible, including Mary and Joseph's marriage, were match-made; yet critics say that match-making is outdated.

Let it be known that the Holy Bible can never be outdated. The Word of God is always new, and Jesus is the same yesterday, today and forever. The scripture is given to us for doctrine, corrections and reproofs; and we are to use it until Jesus comes, and even beyond this world. It can never be outdated.

All Scripture is given by inspiration of God, and is profitable for doctrine, for reproof, for correction, for instruction in righteousness.

(2 Timothy 3:16)

Every scripture in the Bible, including match-making, is profitable to us and can never be outdated. However, I am not saying that all marriages should be arranged by matchmaking. What I am saying is that matchmaking is not wrong. You can meet your spouse yourself. There is no problem in that.

Many people have remained unmarried today because they have refused the idea of others being introduced to them for marriage. If you are experiencing difficulty in finding a spouse yourself, a close associate, friend or family member that is a believer can introduce someone to you. If you like the person introduced to you, if he or she is a believer, and you have peace in your heart, then marry him or her.

Matchmaking does not mean the absence of God's guidance; it actually means the absence of your own wisdom. For instance, the matchmaking of Isaac and Rebekah was done through the guidance of God and through the absence of Isaac's wisdom.

There are many people who marry through matchmaking without knowing it. Because some people don't like matchmaking, when introducing an intended spouse to such people it is made to look as if it wasn't planned. Whether it is obviously planned or not, any introduction of a man and a woman with the intention of marriage is matchmaking.

Is interclass marriage wrong?

I have heard many people condemn marriages between men of low-income class and ladies of high-income class. They have attempted to use man's wisdom and human sense of reasoning to explain their point. They have taught that it is wrong for a man to marry a lady who is richer than him. The end result of such teaching is that rich spinsters don't get married on time because the percentage of rich men willing to marry the spinsters is low.

I want you to know that you can get married to any believer irrespective of your social class or status. Let us look at some marriages between low class men and very rich women for you to see that there is nothing wrong in a man marrying a woman that is richer than him.

David, whom God described as a man after His heart got married to the king's daughter as a shepherd boy. David came from a poor family. When he was asked to marry king Saul's daughter, he was very surprised that the king should ask him to marry his daughter who is regarded as the richest spinster in the nation.

And David said unto Saul, Who am I? and what is my life, or my father's family in Israel, that I should be son in law to the king?

(1 Samuel 18:18)

In the verse above, David clearly stated that his father's family and his life are worth nothing. This verse makes us know that David was nobody at the time he married the king's daughter. David at that time belonged to the lowest class and got married to the king's daughter that belonged to the highest class in their nation. There are other verses that best explain the class of David before he got married to the king's daughter.

> *And Saul commanded his servants, saying, Commune with David secretly, and say, Behold, the king had delight in thee, and all his servants love thee: now therefore be the king's son in law.*
> *And Saul's servants spoke those words in the ears of David. And David said, Seemeth it to you a light thing to be a king's son in law, seeing that I am a poor man and lightly esteemed?*
>
> (1 Samuel 18:22-23)

From the verses above, you will see David saying that he is a poor man and lightly esteemed. I believe these descriptions best suit the lowest class any person could be in. To be *lightly esteemed* means he is not regarded at all, and combining it with poverty means that

David's social class was very low.

Irrespective of his very low class, David still got married to Michal the king's daughter who could be regarded as the spinster of the highest class since her father was a very rich king. Any Christian man can marry any Christian lady irrespective of the difference in their social classes.

Smith Wigglesworth also married a wife of a higher class. Smith Wigglesworth came from a very poor family and was uneducated before he got married to his wife, Pony. His family was so poor that they couldn't afford his school fees, and for that reason he started an apprenticeship in plumbing at the age of six. In his late teens, just as he was about becoming a master plumber, he met Pony and they got married. It was after their marriage that he learned English as his wife taught him the Bible. The great work of God that Smith Wigglesworth did in Christendom will never be forgotten.

If you put Smith Wigglesworth's ministry into consideration, you will say that he had a good marriage. Yet his wife was of a higher social class before their marriage.

There is nothing wrong in a man marrying a woman that is richer than him or a woman of a higher social status. Some critics say that ladies of higher status have the tendency of not being submissive to their husbands. This is not true, as wealth or poverty does not determine whether a lady would be arrogant or disobedient to her husband when married. There are many cases in which poor ladies are not submissive to their husbands. There are also a lot of cases in which rich ladies are submissive to their husbands. Social status or wealth is not a determinant of who will make a good or bad wife. What matters most is that the man and the woman are true believers.

Is it wrong for a man to marry an older lady?

The scripture does not specify any age difference between the man and the woman as a condition for marriage. The man being older or younger than the woman, or both of them being of the same age does not affect the success of their marriage. What is important is that the man and the woman must be adults. Marriage is a union between two adults.

Age difference is not enough reason to cancel a marriage to somebody you have already chosen. There are cases where a man finds a lady he likes and believes they can live as husband and wife, only to discover that the lady is older than him, and for that reason, cancels his proposed marriage to her.

Age does not determine whether a woman is bad or good. Age does not also determine how successful a marriage will be. In fact, in most cases older ladies are more mature and tolerant than younger ones. But that does not mean a lot of young ladies are not mature. In essence, I am saying that age difference is irrelevant to having a successful marriage. What is relevant is that both the man and the woman are true believers.

When God directs the steps of true believers to meet and they like each other, age difference is not enough reason to stop them from getting married.

CHAPTER TEN

My Testimony: I Got Married Within 21 Days of Finding My Wife

*I*n the year 1996, I decided to get married. I was of age and very comfortable financially. So I began to look for the right spouse. I was very careful in my search because I never wanted to make a mistake in my choice of spouse. I was praying to God, asking Him to find a wife for me. Then I didn't know God could only direct a spouse my way. I thought God could also make a choice for me. What a mistake! This mistake cost me six long years of waiting supposedly on the Lord. Those six years were very long and terrible. How I waited and yearned for a miracle to come my way.

On the 1st of January 2002, in making my

New Year resolution, I decreed that I would be getting married on my birthday of that same year, the 17th of August 2002. This declaration was wholly based on faith because at that time I had not found anyone I wanted to marry. I still did not find anyone until the 26th of July 2002, 21 days to my birthday.

On that fateful day, the persistent ringing of the phone woke me up at about 10:00 am. I had attended a night vigil service the previous night and I came back home at about 6:00 am. I had barely slept for 4 hours when the phone started ringing. The call was from one of my employees informing me that I needed to attend to some vital matters in the office.

Just as I finished attending to the matters in the office, my sister and brother, Kate and Henry walked in. Quickly, I told them I had settled the issue of how to find my spouse. At the night vigil service, I was convinced I had an encounter with God concerning finding my spouse. I prayed that God would direct my right spouse to meet me in my office. I was very convinced my prayers were answered and I decided I would not worry any longer about whom to marry. So I told them that my right spouse would visit me in my office. They were stunned.

After a while, Henry asked me about Uche.

Uche, at that time was only a family friend and a true born again Christian. When I first met her the previous year, I had thought of the possibility of getting married to her. But I cancelled the idea when she didn't attend my birthday celebration on the 17th of August 2001. I felt she failed to attend my birthday celebration because she didn't care about me. Though she came the next day with a birthday card, I thought the right thing to do was to forget about the relationship. And that I did.

After that event, she relocated to Enugu, a city in the eastern part of Nigeria. We lost contact. I was truly surprised when my brother asked me about her. So I told him I had not seen her for about a year. I was still speaking when I heard a knock on the door. The door opened and Uche walked in. Instantly, I beheld the most beautiful girl on earth standing by my office door.

I began to wonder why I hadn't taken note of her brilliant beauty long before then. I was so excited and surprised that I could not even propose to her. Before I realised it, she was gone. Till date, that is still one of the shortest visits I have ever had.

The Bible makes it clear that you will have peace of mind when you make the right decision because the Holy Spirit lives inside of you. Conversely, you will not have peace in your heart when you make the wrong decision.

> *Great peace have they who love your law,*
> *and nothing can make them stumble.*
>   (Psalm 119:165 NIV)

If you are born again, this peace in your heart shall guide you in knowing whether you are making the right choice or not. Before I found my wife, I was always seeking for people's opinions to know if a lady would make a good wife or not. Many men do this too. After I saw Uche that day, I did not seek any more opinion because I had peace in my heart. So, I told my close friends and relatives that I had finally found my wife.

When she left, I went home and bought some drinks. I called in some friends to rejoice with me. In the course of the celebration, a friend of mine asked if I had proposed to Uche. He then advised me to propose and get her approval first before celebrating because someone else might have proposed to her.

Fear almost gripped me but I insisted that she is my wife and that no one else can marry her. If I had accepted that thought, perhaps, I might not have married Uche. As I was to learn later that someone else had proposed to her.

Uche left Lagos for Enugu the day after she came to my office. So, I immediately called and proposed marriage to her. She told me someone else had just proposed to her. Without wasting time, I travelled to Enugu, a seven-hour journey by road, to discuss with her at length. She did not give me her consent that day but I was happy that I had a better understanding of the situation. I was happy because I then knew how to channel my prayers. I prayed really fervently. I was also combining my faith with work. I was travelling from Lagos to Enugu regularly. Sometimes, I would come back that same day, and sometimes the next day.

Then finally, one day, she told me she wanted to pray about it. Some men of God also joined her in praying about it. Since God is not an author of confusion, they all had peace in their hearts about the decision of Uche and I getting married. It was on the 7th of August 2002 at Enugu that Uche accepted my marriage proposal.

I went on to suggest that we should get married on the 17th of August, which was only 10 days away. Since I had already decreed I would get married on my birthday, it was important to me that I got married on the 17th of August. Uche's family saw it as a deliberate discourtesy, in the sense that the date was too soon.

However, because they were believers, they went down on their knees and prayed to God for guidance. After praying to God, Uche's family agreed that we could get married on the 17th of August. Ultimately, Uche and I got married on my birthday, the 17th day of August 2002; exactly three weeks from the day I met her in my office. I give all the glory to the Lord God Almighty who made it possible.

It is worthy of note that I did not go through a courtship relationship with Uche before getting married to her because I was sure God directed her steps to me. I trusted God's guidance and we got married without courtship. My marriage to Uche, besides my receiving and accepting Christ as my personal Saviour, is the best thing that has happened to me. Just like Adam said, I can proudly and truly say: *she is now bone of my bones and flesh of my flesh.*

CHAPTER ELEVEN

Advice for Single Men

And the LORD God said, It is not good that the man should be alone; I will make him an help meet for him.

(Genesis 2:18)

*T*he above passage clearly shows that God desires every man to be married. He even promised a reward for anyone who gets married. To such a person, He will bestow favour. The Scripture says: *Whoso findeth a wife findeth a good thing, and obtaineth favour of the LORD* (Proverbs 18:22). For God to give a special reward for marriage shows He has a passionate desire to see that every man gets married.

Irrespective of the fact that God desires that every man should be married, many men are afraid of getting married. Men are afraid for such

117

reasons as the financial commitment involved, the possibility of making the wrong choice, and so on. No matter your position in the church or how prayerful you may be, the truth is that if you are afraid of getting married, you do not have faith in God. No matter how you look at it, you need to overcome your fears because they indicate lack of faith in God.

Here are some important counsel to help you overcome your fears and get married to your right spouse.

What is the basic financial requirement for a man before marriage?

There are many men who do not want to get married until they become very rich. In some cases, it may take them years to make the kind of money they need before they get married. Some end up not even making the money.

The truth is that you don't need excess money to get married; rather you need marriage to make excess money. The principal financial requirement for a man before marriage is to have a job that gives him a basic salary, no matter how small. It is very important that you have a regular source of income. If you are operating your own business, ensure you make a steady income no matter how little.

Once you have a job, you can get married. When you are married, God says, you have found a good thing and you will obtain favour from Him. The marriage will not only increase the level of God's favour upon your life, it will also increase your spiritual strength. The combination of the increased favour from God and increased spiritual strength will result in your making excess money when you go about it the right way.

How to finance a marriage ceremony with a low budget

Financing marriage ceremonies and weddings in some parts of the world especially in Africa can be very expensive. This has led to many late marriages. In some cases, the men find their right spouse, but are not able to get married because of the huge cost of financing marriage ceremonies. I must quickly say at this stage that the cost of a marriage ceremony is not enough reason to stop any person from getting married. I have come to realise that no matter how low your budget is; you can successfully get married. All you need to do is to invite a small number of persons for the marriage ceremony to suit your budget.

If your budget for the marriage ceremony is very low, you can also limit your marriage ceremony to the payment of bride price or dowry. The Bible recognises that the couple is legally married when bride price or dowry is paid. All you need to do after payment of the bride price or dowry is to take your wife to your pastor for marriage blessing.

You must realise that the ceremony of marriage is not more important than marriage itself. It is only a means to the marriage. Marriage itself is what matters most. **Every man should desire to get married by all means.** Whether the budget for your marriage ceremony is high or low, it is important that you get married. Once you get married, you will begin to experience fresh favour from God and your financial level must increase.

How to raise funds to finance your marriage ceremony

God is the most important source of funds for your marriage ceremony. You can only raise the funds from God by asking Him in prayers. He is ever willing to sponsor your marriage ceremony. If He gives reward to people for getting married, then He will be more than glad to sponsor your marriage ceremony, only if you would ask him. He is always willing to provide resources for the marriage ceremony of His children. An example of such willingness is seen in chapter 2 of the book of John, where Jesus turned water into wine.

Jesus, his mother and his disciples attended a marriage ceremony at Cana in Galilee. From the scripture, you will see that the celebrants had a very low budget for the marriage ceremony. Apart from the available drinks not being enough, the drinks were of inferior quality.

And when they wanted wine, the mother of Jesus saith unto him, They have no wine.
(John 2:3)

The above passage clearly indicates there was not enough drink for the invited guests in the marriage ceremony. Also in verse 10, after Jesus had turned water into wine, the governor of the feast commented that the bridegroom brought the inferior quality first before bringing the good wine.

And saith unto him, Every man at the beginning doth set forth good wine; and when men have well drunk, then that

> *which is worse: but thou hast kept the*
> *good wine until now.*
>
> (John 2:10)

For the celebrant to serve inferior quality wine that wasn't even enough for the invited guest means that his budget for the marriage ceremony was very low. Yet because Jesus appeared on the scene, the deficiency that was experienced in the marriage ceremony was transformed to abundance. Not only did Jesus make wine available in the marriage ceremony, the quality of the wine he made was so good that it drew the attention of the governor of the feast. All you need to do if you want to raise funds for your marriage ceremony is to invite Our Lord into your marriage just like the bridegroom in Cana invited Jesus to his marriage – and he had abundance. Invite Him in prayer.

He is ever willing to sponsor your marriage ceremony if you would ask Him. Because it is more important to God that you get married than it is to you, He will go to any length to make sure you have a successful marriage ceremony. He will even break protocols to make sure you have a befitting marriage ceremony, just like Jesus broke protocols so that the marriage ceremony in Cana would be a success.

*Jesus saith unto her, Woman, what have I
to do with thee? Mine hour is not yet come.*
(John 2:4)

When the mother of Jesus complained to
Jesus that there was no more wine in the marriage ceremony, Jesus told her that his time had
not yet come. **Truly, his time to perform mir-
acles had not come, but because of God's
willingness to provide resources for marriage ceremonies, our master Jesus Christ
had to turn water into wine.** He broke the
protocol and turned water into wine. I want
you to know that if you are a Christian, the
same Jesus Christ who turned water into wine
lives in you and will ensure that you have the
required resources for your marriage ceremony
– if you ask him.

Once you ask God to assist you in raising
funds for your marriage ceremony, He will
answer your prayer. He can provide you the
funds directly or he can favour you in your work.
He can also raise funds for you through people
giving you money as gifts or through other
means. **No matter the means, the most important thing is that God will always provide
resources for your marriage ceremony.**

Is it good to borrow funds to finance your marriage ceremony?

You must never borrow money – even a dime – to finance your wedding. If you borrow money to finance your marriage ceremony, would you also borrow to take care of your family after marriage? Moreover, if you borrow money for your marriage ceremony, you will need to pay back afterwards. The time you would have spent in building your family would then be used in looking for money to pay back the loan. If you are collecting money from any body, let it be as gift and not as loan.

> *For the LORD thy God blesseth thee, as he promised thee: and thou shalt lend unto many nations, but thou shalt not borrow...*
>
> (Deuteronomy 15:6)

Rather than borrowing money, it is better to adjust your marriage ceremony to suit the amount of money you have.

You must never marry an unbeliever

Though I have treated this topic in the preceding chapters, I deem it necessary to briefly revisit it here. It is not permitted in the kingdom for anyone to marry an unbeliever.

> *Be ye not unequally yoked together with unbelievers: for what fellowship has righteousness with unrighteousness? and what communion hath light with darkness?*
> *And what concord has Christ with Belial? or what part hath he that believeth with an infidel?*
> *And what agreement hath the temple of God with idols? for ye are the temple of the living God; as God hath said, I will dwell in them and walk in them; and I will be their God, and they shall be my people.*
> *Wherefore, come out from among them, and be ye separate, saith the Lord, and touch not the unclean thing; and I will receive you.*
>
> (2 Corinthians 6:14-17)

From the above scripture, you will understand that it is not permissible for a believer to marry an unbeliever. There is also a curse on anyone who marries an unbeliever.

Do not intermarry with them. Do not give your daughters to their sons or take their daughters for your sons, for they will turn your sons away from following me to serve other gods, and the LORD's anger will burn against you and will quickly destroy you.

(Deuteronomy 7:3 NIV)

Can I convert an unbeliever and marry her?

Marriage to an unbeliever is not at all entertained in the kingdom. It is also wrong to convert an unbeliever for the purpose of marrying her. There is the tendency that the lady will pretend to accept Christ just for the purpose of getting married to you. This should not be overlooked. I am not saying that it is wrong to marry a girl you brought into Christ. If the Lord uses you to convert a lady and afterwards you decide to marry her, there is nothing wrong with that.

...know thou the God of thy father, and serve him with a perfect heart and with a willing mind: for the LORD searcheth all hearts, and understandeth all the imaginations of the thoughts...

(1 Chronicles 28:9)

Do no convert an unbeliever for the purpose of marrying her.

How to choose your right spouse

Because of the importance and purpose of marriage, you must never leave God out of your plans. Marrying without God's direction is like marrying through a lucky dip – you may marry the right spouse or you may not. Your choice of spouse will be based on chance. You will not be sure if your spouse is the right one until you have married her. But when you marry with God's direction, it will not be a marriage of chance because God who knows the end before the beginning knows the right spouse for you. You will be sure to get married to your right spouse and enjoy your marriage. In as much as God will never choose a particular spouse for you, He will direct her to you, like He brought Eve to Adam and brought Rebekah to Abraham's servant.

For God to direct your steps to your right spouse, you must ask Him in prayer just like Abraham's servant prayed when he was looking for a wife for Isaac. When God directs your spouse to you, there is no mistake whatsoever in getting married to that person because God sees the outcome of a marriage even before it begins.

Note that in as much as God directs your intended spouse to you, the decision to get married to that person lies with you and not with God. God does not interfere with our right of choice. Once God directs a true believer to you and you like her, go ahead and marry her without further delay. God cannot make a mistake; neither can He deceive you. I challenge you to make a move now and get married. My earnest prayer and desire is that you should get married to your right spouse without further delay, in Jesus name. Amen.

CHAPTER TWELVE

Advice for Single Ladies

*Y*ou are fearfully and wonderfully created. Do you know that you are very special to God? Do you know that you were not formed from the ground like men were formed?

> *And the LORD God caused a deep sleep to fall upon Adam, and he slept: and he took one of his ribs, and closed up the flesh instead thereof;*
> *And the rib, which the Lord God had taken from man, made he a woman, and brought her unto the man.*
>
> (Genesis 2:21-22)

You are very special and you must see yourself as a special and beautiful person. Having known you are special, I enjoin you never to be desperate in getting married. No man ever wants to get married to a desperate woman. Some ladies have the wrong notion that time is not on their side. They become so desperate that they are even willing to get married to unbelievers.

Please never make the mistake of marrying an unbeliever. Time is not against you. I have attended a wedding of a 52-year-old woman. That will not be your portion in Jesus Name, Amen. But I want you to know that time is never against you at all. Desperation puts men off. If you have the major qualities men want, you will be married to the man you desire without delay.

Major qualities men want in ladies

You must have a humble disposition. Every man wants a humble lady that will respect him when they get married. You must be able to let everybody that comes around you know that you are humble.

> *...God resisteth the proud, but giveth grace unto the humble.*
>
> (James 4:6)

Every man wants to be in charge. If a man is not sure you will be under his control, he will not get married to you. This fear is common in men, especially when the lady's educational, financial or family background intimidate them. You must be humble enough to be married by a man.

Another important quality a man wants in a lady is faithfulness, a lady that will never commit sexual sin all the days of her life. I have come to realise that over 98% of born-again men have one major fear, the fear of choosing an unfaithful life partner. No man ever wants to share his wife with someone else. Every man is afraid of getting married to a loose woman. Man by nature is very possessive and this is not very surprising, since God is a jealous God.

> *Thou shall not bow down thyself to them, nor serve them: for I the LORD your God am a jealous God...*
>
> (Exodus 20:5)

Every man wants to have his wife to himself and for himself alone. To most men, this is most important. They can share everything else but their wives. They are ready to entertain every other thing but the infidelity of their wives. This is why many a man never marries a lady he has slept with because he feels that the lady would also sleep with other men just like she slept with him. It is so important to a man that even in some cases the lady may not be promiscuous but because the man doesn't trust her, he refuses to marry her. Apart from not committing sexual sins, it is also very important that you are trusted in the area of fidelity. I will let you know what to do in order to make men trust you in this area.

How to make a man trust in your fidelity

You should surrender yourself totally to Christ and His work. Every man knows that a **true** born-again Christian will never sleep with any person except her husband. Based on the human will power, it is difficult. But if you are a **true** born again, it is settled – you will never sleep with another person except your husband. Every man knows this and that is why men, including unbelievers, desire to marry true born-again Christians.

Your level of commitment in your local church determines the level of love you have for God. The level of love you have for God in turn determines how true a believer you are. You should be highly devoted to the work of God in your local church and in the kingdom of God in general.

You must never feign commitment to God's work. If you are not sincere, it will be known because it is not from your heart. If you have been pretending or you have not been totally committed to God's work, all you need to do now is to re-dedicate your life to Christ and become fully devoted to His work.

You don't have to change your local church for you to be noticed by an intended spouse. Continue to work for God devotedly in your local church, the man will find you. If the man does not find you, someone else will discover you and tell him.

Another conscious step you must take in making men trust you in the area of extra-marital relationship is never to be involved in pre-marital sex. If you sleep with one person, the news will unfailingly get to many others. You should know that men gossip more than women in this area. Some men boast about it, while some repentantly confess to their friends.

You must deliberately abstain from sex before marriage. When you get married, you will have your husband to sleep with all the days of your life. You must never indulge in pre-marital sex.

Can a man take fire in his bosom, and his clothes not be burned?
Can one go upon hot coals, and his feet not be burned?

(Proverbs 6:27-28)

Finally you must take your husband by force. You must pray fervently and command your kind of man to propose to you.

And from the days of John the Baptist until now, the kingdom of heaven suffereth violence, and the violent take it by force.

(Matthew 11:12)

The Bible says: *none shall lack her mate* (Isaiah 34:16). Use the scripture to command your mate to come forth. If you follow my counsel and pray fervently with faith, your right spouse will come to you and propose without further delay, in Jesus Name. Amen!

① Lord your Love to me
② You made me so beautiful
③ Choir ; LEAVE it for God

From ~~Unibeg~~ take a bus
~~to~~ next bus-stop after
Unibeg is Chambers
Stop there and oppos
there you will see
Federal college of
Education, enter the
gate and ask the
~~go~~ gateman .